PIONEERS OF SCIENCE

MICHAEL FARADAY

Michael Brophy

Wayland

Pioneers of Science

Archimedes
Alexander Graham Bell
Karl Benz
Marie Curie
Michael Faraday
Leonardo da Vinci
Guglielmo Marconi
Isaac Newton

Series editor Rosemary Ashley
Designer David Armitage

First published in 1990 by
Wayland (Publishers) Limited
61 Western Road, Hove
East Sussex BN3 1JD, England

© 1990 Wayland (Publishers) Limited

British Library Cataloguing in Publication Data
Brophy, Michael
   Michael Faraday.
   1. Physics. Faraday, Michael, 1791–1867
   I. Title II. Series
   530.092

   ISBN 1–85210–956–4

Typeset by Nicola Taylor, Wayland
Printed in Italy by Rotolito Lombarda S.p.A.
Bound in France by A.G.M.

Contents

1 ▽ First Steps as a Scientist

When we think of a scientist today we usually have a picture in our minds of a man or a woman in a white coat working in a laboratory with chemicals and scientific equipment. Two hundred years ago that was not how scientists thought of themselves. Most of them were fairly rich men who studied science as a hobby. They did not earn their living as scientists but enjoyed thinking about the problems of science and trying to work out ideas and theories in their heads. They attended meetings where these different ideas were discussed, and wrote to other people interested in science. They preferred to call themselves 'thinkers' or 'philosophers' rather than scientists.

The library of the Royal Institution in London. The Institution was founded in 1799 with the aim of spreading scientific knowledge and 'teaching the application of science to the common purposes of life'.

The house in Jacob's Well Mews where Faraday lived as a boy.

Things were beginning to change by 1800 and one man, in particular, helped speed up the change. Because of his background and his approach to science he has probably had more effect on our modern image of a scientist than anyone else. His name was Michael Faraday.

Faraday was born in 1791 in the village of Newington in Surrey, now part of London. His father, a blacksmith, had moved there from the north of England shortly before Michael's birth, hoping to find more work. Unfortunately, Michael's father became ill and was unable to earn much money. So there was little to spare for education and when the boy left school at thirteen he knew nothing about science. All he had studied was reading, writing and a little mathematics. Later, when he was a famous scientist, he still felt that he was not very good at mathematics.

As soon as he left school, Michael got a job as a messenger boy in a book shop. He had to deliver books and newspapers around the streets of London and do odd jobs for the owner of the shop. He must have been a good worker, for after only one year the owner, George Riebau, offered to train him as a bookbinder. Most people had to pay for a training in those days but Mr Riebau gave Michael a free apprenticeship.

The apprenticeship lasted seven years and it was during this time that Michael became interested in science. Customers would often bring in books and magazines to be bound in leather covers. The young apprentice helped to do this but often he was more interested in what was inside the books. When he was older he told friends how he used to love reading the scientific books that came into the shop. Mr Riebau even allowed him to make copies of the most interesting ones.

George Riebau's bookshop where Faraday was apprenticed as a bookbinder.

Humphry Davy was an excellent speaker and his lectures did much to make science popular. Here he is seen lecturing at the Royal Institution.

As well as training to become a bookbinder, Michael took art and drawing lessons from an artist. He did not earn enough to pay for the lessons, so instead he used to clean and tidy the artist's house. He also started to attend talks and lectures on science. Sometimes his older brother gave him the money he needed to get in to the lecture hall. He took detailed notes of the lectures he attended and then bound them into books. Mr Riebau showed some of these notes to one of his customers who was a member of an important scientific institution, the Royal Institution of London. The customer, Mr Dance, was so impressed that he bought the young man a set of tickets for a series of lectures at the Royal Institution. The talks were to be given by a famous scientist, Sir Humphry Davy.

Michael Faraday was delighted. It was his first chance to listen to a really important scientist. He had finished his seven-year apprenticeship and was now a qualified bookbinder, but he was full of enthusiasm for science and he wanted, somehow, to become a scientist himself. After the lectures he wrote to Sir Humphry Davy and sent him a well-bound copy of the notes he had taken at the lectures. Davy was impressed and invited Michael to come and meet him at the Royal Institution. But he advised him not to leave his job as a bookbinder because it was almost impossible to earn a living as a scientist. Michael was disappointed but still determined to become a scientist.

Since finishing his apprenticeship he had taken a new job as a qualified bookbinder at another bookshop. The owner, Mr De La Roche, was a friend of Mr Riebau and like his friend thought highly of the young man's work. He told him, 'I have no child, and if you will stay with me you shall have all when I am gone.' In spite of this good offer, Michael knew that he wanted to devote himself to science. Then something happened which completely changed his life.

Sir Humphry Davy had been working on an experiment in his laboratory when it exploded. Glass and hot chemicals showered around him and damaged his eyes. He was unable to continue with his work by himself, so he asked Faraday to help him until his eyes recovered. The young man seized the opportunity, and only regretted that it was no more than a temporary job. He would have to go back to bookbinding when Davy's sight returned to normal.

The Royal Institution in Albermarle Street. It had a lecture theatre and science laboratories as well as a library and quickly became an important scientific centre.

Michael Faraday's study at the Royal Institution.

A few months later the laboratory assistant at the Royal Institution had an argument with another worker and hit him. The assistant, William Payne, was sacked for fighting. Davy proposed that the job should be offered to Michael Faraday. Even though he would earn a lot less as an assistant than as a qualified bookbinder, he accepted the offer and on 1 March 1813, very proudly became the chemistry assistant at the Royal Institution. He was allowed to live in rooms in the Royal Institution and so could save money, but more importantly he had taken his first step towards becoming a real scientist.

As Davy's assistant, Faraday carried out his orders and helped him with his experiments. It certainly was not a quiet or easy job. In letters to his friends he described what it was like. 'I have been engaged this afternoon in assisting Sir Humphry in his experiments. . . during which we had two or three unexpected explosions.'

In another letter he wrote, 'I have escaped (not quite unhurt) from four different strong explosions.'

And later he wrote again, 'I met with another explosion on Saturday evening which has again laid up my eyes.'

2 A Trip to Europe

In 1813 Michael Faraday was a laboratory assistant but he was still a long way from being a famous scientist. When he first started, there were two other laboratory assistants working in the Royal Institution with him. They both left for other jobs. Faraday might easily have done the same and returned to bookbinding. Or he might simply have remained as an assistant to Davy. But he had a second stroke of good luck. Shortly after he was appointed, Davy arranged to go on a long trip to Europe. He intended to meet and talk with many of the most famous scientists there and he invited his assistant to go along with him.

They set off in October 1813: Sir Humphry, his wife, and Michael Faraday his assistant. The first country they visited was France. The only piece of bad luck for Faraday was that at the last minute Davy's servant refused to travel. He had fled from France during the French Revolution and was afraid to return, because England was at war with France. This meant that Faraday had to do many of the jobs the servant would normally have done.

Faraday had asked Davy if it was safe to go to France with the war on. Sir Humphry's answer was, 'War has nothing to do with science.'

This seems an unusual idea to us now that science has so much to do with war. Guided missiles, atomic weapons, spy satellites, the latest aircraft, tanks, ships and weapons all depend on scientists for their design and development. But in Davy's time science was still seen mainly as a hobby or an interest for rich people. Sir Humphry proved to be right for no one bothered them. In fact Napoleon, the Emperor of France, ordered that the scientist and his party should be treated with great respect and offered any assistance they needed.

Napoleon Bonaparte, Emperor of France 1804–1815, who ordered Davy and his party to be well treated even though France was at war with England.

Although he enjoyed his meetings with famous scientists in Europe, Faraday had problems on the trip. For a start he was not very happy with the local food. He wrote to a friend in England about staying in the best hotel in a small French town and said, 'I think it is impossible for an English person to eat the things that come out of this place.' But his main problem was with Davy's wife. Faraday enjoyed being an assistant to Sir Humphry but he was not happy at having to act as a servant to Lady Davy, especially because of the way she treated him. In a letter to a friend he wrote that she had an 'evil disposition' and that she was 'haughty and proud to an excessive degree', and delighted in 'making her inferiors feel her influence'.

Meetings with leading scientists

During the trip to Europe Faraday met many famous scientists. Among them were Alessandro Volta and André Marie Ampère, who are remembered today because of their work on electricity. Volta, an Italian, had made the first electric battery in 1800. The unit for measuring the strength of a battery or an electric power point, the volt, is named after him.

Ampère's work was in the field of electricity and magnetism, where Faraday later made his own most famous inventions. The ampere, the unit we use for measuring current, is named after Ampère.

Left *Alessandro Volta demonstrating his electric battery to the Emperor Napoleon and members of his court.*

At one time Faraday was so depressed that he wrote, 'I should not hesitate to leave them in any part of the world for I know I could get home as well without them as with them.' However, the work he was doing and the experience of meeting other scientists made up for the humiliation, and so he stayed.

When the party was in Paris, Ampère brought them a small amount of a new substance which French scientists had just succeeded in separating, or extracting, from seaweed. They did not know what it was and asked Davy and Faraday to try to identify it. After a week they were able to announce that it was a completely new substance or element, one we now call iodine. (You may have used it at home as a disinfectant for cuts and scrapes.) When they heard that Davy and Faraday had succeeded, many French scientists were angry with Ampère for giving the two Englishmen the substance and so allowing them the honour of discovering the new element.

Faraday visited a sugar factory like this one while in France. He had extracted sugar from beet in his laboratory and wanted to see the process at work in a factory.

13

Davy's party had to cross the Alps to get into Switzerland. As this engraving shows, passage through the Alpine passes was difficult at the best of times.

After Paris the party set out for Switzerland but they had to cross the Alps and the roads were blocked with snow. Davy was determined to keep going and arranged for sixty-five men to walk in front of the carriage to clear the way and to lift the vehicle whenever it became stuck. Even when they came to the end of the road he refused to be beaten. He ordered the men to dismantle the carriage and load it on to sledges and mules. And so they set off again, with Sir Humphry and Faraday walking and Lady Davy being carried in a sedan chair. Faraday carried a barometer in his hands so that he could measure how the atmospheric pressure dropped as they climbed higher and higher.

From Switzerland the party went on to Italy and visited the Grand Duke of Tuscany. The Duke had built a large telescope and Sir Humphry was keen to use it in an experiment to burn a diamond. Using the telescope, he focused rays of light from the sun onto the diamond and watched it burn away. Faraday recorded that, 'The diamond gave off intense heat and a beautiful scarlet light.' He also noted that, 'The experiment was repeated several times.' Davy was clearly a very wealthy man.

From Tuscany they went to Naples and climbed the volcano Vesuvius. We are told that they sat on top of the volcano and cooked eggs in the heat from the molten lava. But for all the adventures and the meetings with famous scientists, both Davy and Faraday were becoming tired of travelling and decided to return home early. 'I fancy that when I set my foot in England I shall never take it out again,' wrote Faraday to a friend.

Mount Vesuvius near Naples, in Italy, pictured in 1825, a few years after Davy and Faraday visited it.

3 Faraday's Early Discoveries

Back in London Faraday continued to work as an assistant to Davy at the Royal Institution. He worked with him on his most famous invention, the miner's safety lamp.

In the early 1800s there was a great increase in the demand for coal. More and more mines were opened to meet the need but there were many accidents. The mines were underground and in the dark so the miners had to use lamps. These lamps were very dangerous because they ignited, or set alight, a gas called methane, or 'fire damp', which collected in the mines. Sir Humphry developed a special safety lamp which could give out light without igniting the methane gas around

Opposite An artist's impression of Humphry Davy trying out his safety lamp.

Left Three commercial safety lamps from about 1816. The centre lamp has a 'bull's eye' lens to focus the dim light which the lamp produced.

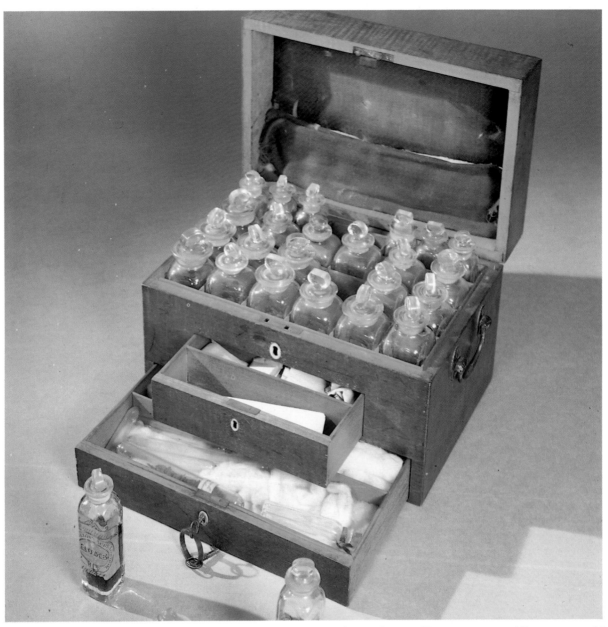

Faraday's chemical cabinet. Although he is best remembered for his work in electricity, Faraday also made important discoveries in chemistry.

it. It saved many lives. Later Davy wrote, 'I am myself indebted to Mr Michael Faraday for much able assistance in the prosecution of my experiments.'

Faraday was still employed as Sir Humphry's assistant but he also began to work on experiments of his own. In 1820 he was responsible for producing some new chemicals. They were compounds made from the gas chlorine and from carbon. One of them we call carbon tetrachloride and nowadays it is used in fire extinguishers and as a stain remover.

Experiments With Steel

Along with a friend called Stodart, Faraday experimented to try to make stainless steel. Iron rusted easily and Faraday and Stodart realized that if they mixed small amounts of other metals with iron they could produce metal alloys which were stronger than iron and less likely to rust. They obtained very good results by mixing small amounts of platinum and silver with the iron but this made the alloy too expensive for ordinary use. The stainless steel that we use today, for razor blades, for sinks and taps (see below) and for knives and forks, was not invented until 1916. But in 1931, another scientist read the notes that Faraday had made a hundred years earlier and found that Faraday and Stodart had made stainless steel long before anyone else. No one at the time had realized how important their discovery was.

Faraday is most famous for his discoveries relating to electricity and magnetism. We shall read about these later but he also carried out experiments in many other areas of science. In 1823 he was the first person in the world to turn chlorine gas into a liquid and in 1824 he discovered the chemical benzene.

In the days before the use of electricity, many houses used gas for lighting. The gas was made by heating whale or fish oil in metal cylinders. When the gas was consumed, it left behind a thick, black, greasy sludge in the cylinders. Faraday was brought some of this sludge and with great patience and skill he was able to isolate a clear, pure liquid. Nowadays we call the liquid benzene. It is a very important chemical in industry and is used in the manufacture of many dyes, perfumes and medicines.

Falcon glass works in Blackfriars, London. Faraday began his investigations of optical glass here (1824–27) before a more convenient furnace was built in the Royal Institution.

Faraday also discovered a new type of glass. He set out to develop special glass for making telescope lenses but instead he developed borosilicate glass. This is the 'heat-proof' glass used to make casserole and glass dishes which can safely be placed in an oven. We also use it for laboratory test-tubes and beakers.

Faraday achieved his ambition and became a famous scientist. He was appointed editor of the Royal Institution's prestigious magazine of science. He lectured at the Royal Institution and at the Military Academy in Woolwich. In 1836 he became the scientific adviser to Trinity House, the association which was responsible for all the lighthouses and lightships around Britain. He also became the scientific adviser to the British Navy and carried out many experiments and tests for them. For example he

Trinity House, Tower Hill. Faraday was scientific adviser to this organization, which is responsible for matters relating to British navigation.

The Royal Military Academy in Woolwich, where Faraday was scientific adviser.

tested the use of different disinfectants and different ways of preserving wood in water. He worked on ways of preventing the ropes on ships from catching fire and even carried out tests to see if ships could be powered by gas. At one stage he was given different samples of porridge meal to test and he found that many of them contained powdered chalk. In order to make bigger profits, dishonest dealers were adding chalk to the oats, so that the sailors at the time were getting a mixture of oats and chalk in their porridge.

As Faraday's reputation as a scientist grew, honours were given to him from many countries. He was awarded an honorary degree from Oxford University. He was appointed a member of the French and of the Swedish Academies of Science. He was honoured by the Swiss, presented with a medal by the King of Prussia and awarded the Medal of Honour by the Emperor of France.

4 Michael Faraday the Man

What type of man was this famous scientist who was honoured by so many countries? People who knew him described Faraday as kind and gentle but very proud. He loved children although he and his wife Sarah never had any of their own. From what we know about him he seems to have been a little eccentric. For example, one story tells how he loved being out in thunderstorms so much that, if he saw there was a storm in another part of London, he would catch a cab to get to it. His wife once wrote to friends that even when he was ill he thought 'nothing of walking thirty miles in a day and one day he walked forty-five miles'.

Religion was very important to Faraday. He belonged to a small Protestant sect called the Sandemanians. They lived their lives strictly according to the Bible and stressed the importance of living and working in a community or group. The sect was named after its founder Robert Sandeman, who had left the Presbyterian Church because he disagreed with its rules. He thought that a church should be governed only by the Bible and not by rules or laws made by people.

An early photograph showing Faraday with his wife, Sarah.

A photograph of John Tyndall, Sarah Faraday, Michael Faraday and Jane Barnard, Faraday's niece.

Faraday believed very strongly that his life and work were guided by God. Even his scientific ideas were based on the belief that there was a single God who created and kept everything in order. John Tyndall, a close friend of Faraday, wrote, 'I think that a good deal of Faraday's week-day strength and persistency might be referred to his Sunday exercises.'

However, Faraday was not a person who could be led easily or be told what to do. He decided for himself what was right or wrong. In 1840 he became an elder, or senior member, of his Church. A few years later he was invited to dine with Queen Victoria on a Sunday. The church members expected him to refuse the invitation and to attend the Sunday service with them as usual. Faraday dined with the Queen. He was dismissed as an elder of the Church and cut off from membership. It was many years before he was readmitted and even longer before he was allowed to become an elder again.

The young Queen Victoria in 1840. By attending dinner with the Queen on a Sunday, Faraday lost his position as an elder of the Sandemanian Church.

When we look back at the life of someone as famous as Michael Faraday it is difficult to think of him or her as an ordinary person. But Faraday had human weaknesses. He became ill like everyone else and he worried about what other people thought and said about him. Although he was friendly with many famous foreign scientists, he displayed some prejudice against people of other nations. In one of his letters he complained about French people chattering and talking too much and wrote that they 'must be a very thinking race to have so much to say'. He once wrote that he found Italians 'effeminate and idle' and that the Swiss were good-natured but 'great cheats'. He said that he liked Americans even though they were full of 'blustering and arrogance' and that, 'The whole nation seems to me as a little impetuous, ignorant, headstrong child...'

Michael Faraday is not famous or honoured for his skills as a politician. We remember him for his discoveries and work as a scientist. So now we must look at the work for which he is most famous, his discoveries about electricity.

5 ▽ Faraday's Work with Electricity

Today electricity plays an important part in all our lives. We use it at work, at home and even to move around. Up until Faraday's time no one used it. A few scientists enjoyed carrying out tests and experiments in their private laboratories to try to find out what electricity was and what it could do. But no one foresaw much use for it. Gladstone, a famous politician who later became Prime Minister of Britain, could not understand why Michael Faraday was so interested in electricity and asked him, 'But, after all, what use is it?' Faraday made a joke that some day the government would be able to tax it, but at that time even he was not able to imagine how important it would become.

Before Faraday's inventions, electricity for scientific experiments was available only from batteries. This giant battery was built in the basement of the Royal Institution by Humphry Davy.

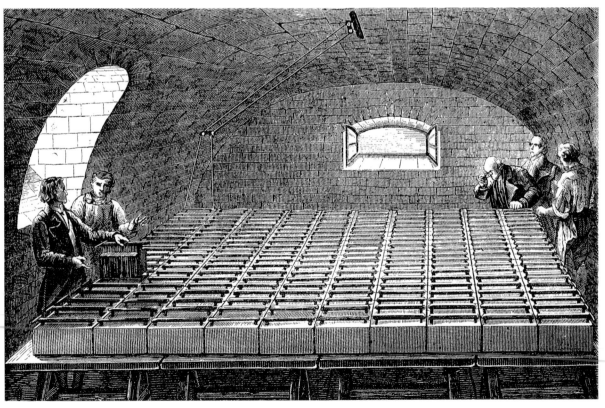

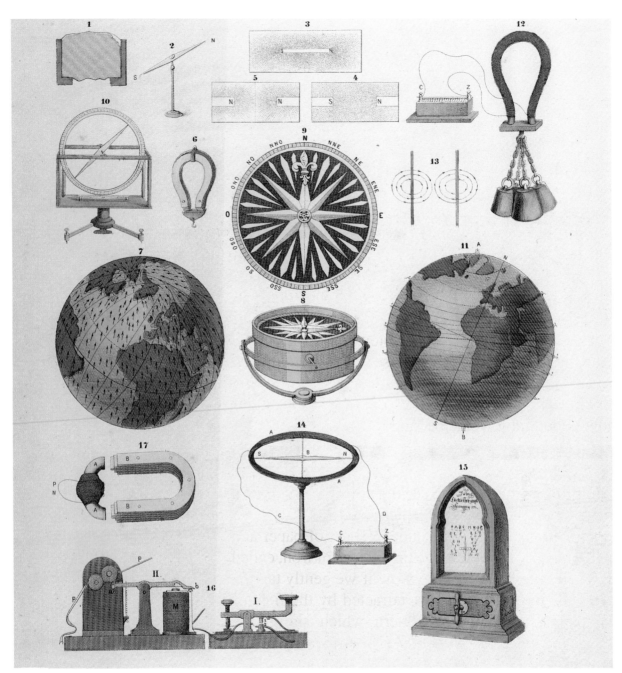

Understanding of magnetism and electricity grew throughout the nineteenth century. This print from 1850 shows magnetic fields (3-5) the power of an electromagnet (12) and Morse telegraph (16).

In 1820 a Danish scientist called Oersted discovered that he could use electricity to produce magnetism. Faraday became interested in Oersted's work and followed everything that he and other scientists wrote about electricity and magnetism. Gradually he became convinced that the power of a magnet was in the space around it rather than in the metal itself and he set out to prove this theory.

It is impossible for us to see the power or 'field' of a magnet but it is easy to get a picture of it. All we need to do is to place a magnet under a sheet of paper and then carefully sprinkle some tiny pieces of iron, called iron filings, on to the paper. Now if we gently tap the paper the iron filings will be attracted by the field of the magnet and form a pattern which shows the magnet's 'lines of force'. As the picture above demonstrates, Faraday was right. The power of a magnet is in the space around it, not inside the magnet.

Faraday was working on these ideas in his laboratory. Right from 1822 he was convinced that he should be able to reverse Oersted's idea. If electricity could be used to produce magnetism, then it should be possible to use magnetism to produce electricity. Faraday carried out over a hundred experiments to try to do this but none of them worked.

This illustration from 1878 shows the pattern formed by lines of magnetic force when iron filings are shaken over a card covering a bar magnet.

The magnetic field of this bar magnet is shown by iron filings scattered on a thin sheet of plastic lying over the magnet. The magnetic force is strongest at the ends, but can be felt all around the magnet.

Early Use for Electricity

In 1825 a scientist called William Sturgeon found a use for electricity. He passed electricity through a wire which was wrapped round an iron bar. The bar became magnetized and was able to lift metals twenty times its own weight. Sturgeon had made the first electromagnet. Today Sturgeon's ideas are used in special cranes which have electromagnets in them to lift huge loads.

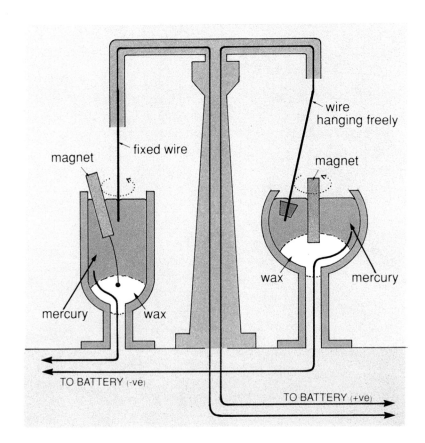

magnet

fixed wire

wire
hanging freely

magnet

wax

mercury

mercury

wax

TO BATTERY (-ve)

TO BATTERY (+ve)

This diagram shows how Faraday produced motion with electromagnetism. On the left a bar magnet in a dish of mercury moves around a fixed wire carrying an electric current. In the right-hand dish, a free wire suspended in mercury moves around the fixed magnet.

Then, in 1830 he came up with a completely new idea. He set up an experiment with a magnet inside a beaker. The cup was filled with a liquid metal called mercury. Faraday connected one end of an electric battery to the bottom of the mercury. Then he connected the other end of the battery to a copper wire. When he allowed the copper wire to hang down into the liquid it began to move. He had found a way of getting electricity and magnetism to work together to produce movement. He had invented the electric motor.

The electric motor was one of the most important inventions in history. We use electric motors at home for stereo players, videos, vacuum cleaners, fans, blenders, drills and lawn-mowers. We use them in cars for starter motors and for windshield wipers, and we use them at work for electric machinery, drills and conveyer belts. So Michael Faraday will always be remembered as the person who invented the first electric motor.

Transformers

The motor was only the starting point for Faraday. A few months later he invented the electric transformer. Every radio, every television, video and cassette player in the world uses this idea. A transformer helps us to use different strengths of electricity. A transistor radio or personal stereo may work using a six-volt battery but if we connect it directly to the 240 volts of an electrical socket it will be destroyed. We can use a transformer to reduce the 240 volts from the mains down to six volts, and then the radio can safely be used.

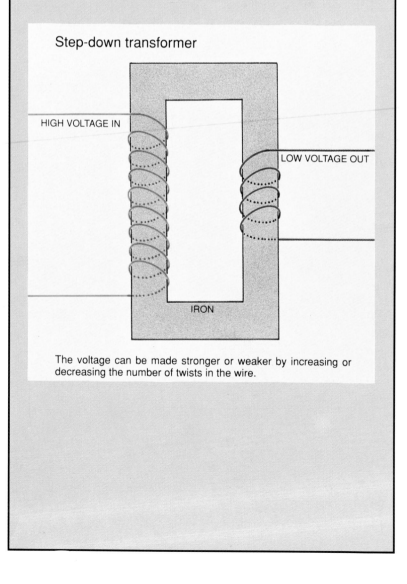

Step-down transformer

HIGH VOLTAGE IN

LOW VOLTAGE OUT

IRON

The voltage can be made stronger or weaker by increasing or decreasing the number of twists in the wire.

Both the electric motor and the transformer work by *using* electricity. But Faraday had still not achieved his ambition of being able to *produce* electricity from magnetism. Then, in October 1831, he finally succeeded. Working in his laboratory at the Royal Institution, he was able to show that when he moved an electrified wire through a magnetic field, electricity was produced. By today's standards the equipment he used was very crude, but Faraday's apparatus was the world's first dynamo. From his simple apparatus, the huge electric generators used in modern power plants have been developed. Faraday's three discoveries, the dynamo, the transformer and the electric motor, made the creation of an electrical industry possible.

Electromagnetic induction: a nineteenth century illustration of how Faraday induced, or made, electricity in a coil. The inner coil is connected to a battery and the outer coil to a galvanometer.

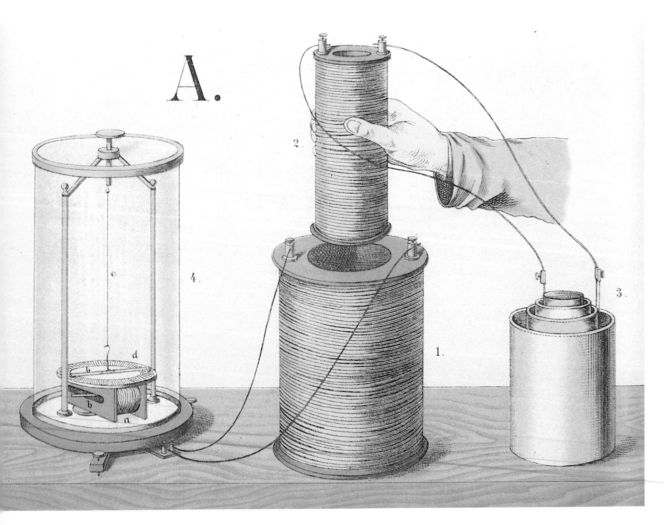

A photograph of Faraday's first dynamo. The copper disc was spun between the poles of the electromagnet, producing a continuous electric current.

Faraday still was not finished with his experiments and discoveries. In 1832 most scientists believed that there were many different types of electricity. They thought that the electricity which came from batteries was different from the electricity that came from dynamos or from electric fish and eels. Faraday disagreed, and carefully and systematically he proved that all these 'different types' of electricity were in fact the same. Electrical energy was the same no matter what source it came from.

Faraday's electroplating apparatus from about 1834. This was used for measuring the electrochemical effects of different sources of electricity.

Next he began to look at how electricity could effect chemicals. He had learnt from Davy that by passing an electric current through certain chemicals, or solutions of certain chemicals in water, he could decompose them or break them down. Faraday was able to show that he could control the breakdown by changing the amount of electricity. From the results of his experiments he proposed a new law for electricity and chemistry. This law stated that, 'Chemical action or decomposing power is exactly proportional to the quantity of electricity'. This law became known as Faraday's First Law and it is still used in industry and appears in almost every basic chemistry book in the world.

Above The electroplating room at a Birmingham metal works in 1844.

'Tin' Cans

We use electroplating to cover one metal with another. For example, iron rusts very easily so we cannot store food in an iron can. But if we cover the iron with a very thin layer of tin, not only does the tin not rust but it stops the iron from rusting as well. And so we can safely store food in the can. Electroplated cans have made it possible for us to store many kinds of foods which would otherwise perish and be unfit to eat.

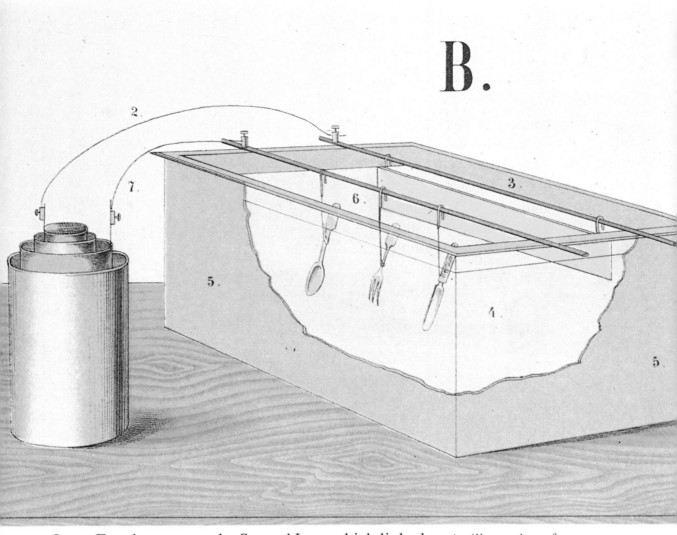

B.

Later Faraday proposed a Second Law which linked the way a chemical was broken down by electricity with the structure of the chemical itself. From Faraday's experiments and his two laws we get all our modern ideas about electroplating.

The electroplating process is used all over the world. Many metal objects such as cutlery, jewellery and the bright metallic parts of cars are electroplated. By doing this an object made from a cheap metal such as iron or copper can be covered with a coating of a more expensive metal such as gold, silver or nickel. The object has the bright attractive appearance of the expensive metal but costs only slightly more than if it was made entirely from the cheap metal.

An illustration of electroplating from a nineteenth century book.

6 **Faraday the Scientist**

Michael Faraday has been called the 'greatest experimentalist who ever lived'. Men and women had certainly been carrying out experiments hundreds and thousands of years before he was born, but Faraday developed the method of testing ideas experimentally much more than anyone before him. He stressed how important it was for scientists never to try to explain something without first checking on the facts through experiments.

Faraday giving a lecture on 'Magnetism and Light' at the Royal Institution in 1846.

Faraday himself would never put forward an idea or theory until he had carefully checked and re-checked the facts. He told a friend, 'Facts are for all times, whilst opinion may change as a cloud in the air.' Once he had an idea for a new theory but did not have the time or opportunity to test it experimentally. He wrote the idea on a piece of paper, sealed it in an envelope and asked that it should be locked in the safe of the Royal Institution. He hoped to have time later to check the facts behind his theory, but, in case anyone else came up with an explanation, he did not want to be accused of stealing their ideas.

Faraday in his laboratory at the Royal Institution, where he carried out thousands of experiments, constantly checking and re-checking his ideas.

Even when he had publicly announced a new idea or theory Faraday was always willing to change his opinion if someone came up with new facts. He told a friend that he was always 'open to conviction'. Once, when he was discussing one of his new ideas, he wrote, 'I have given you this theory not as the true one but as the one which appears true to me and when I perceive errors in it I will immediately renounce it in part or wholly as my judgement may direct.'

In order to check the facts behind his theories Faraday had to carry out enormous numbers of practical experiments and he kept detailed notes and records on all of them. For example, by 1862 he had records of over 16,000 experiments he had carried out on electricity and chemistry.

Faraday was important, therefore, not only because of his own successes but because of the method or scientific approach he used. Not only did he test his own theories through experiment but he encouraged other scientists to follow his example. Writing to a friend he warned him never 'to draw conclusions before every circumstance has been examined'.

Faraday publicly criticized scientists who did not follow this approach. In 1821 he even criticized his friend Ampère. Writing about one of Ampère's theories he noted that, 'Theory makes up the great part of what M. Ampère has published and theory in a great many points unsupported by experiments.'

A few years before he died, Michael Faraday was asked why he thought he had become such a great scientist. He replied, 'I had to work and prepare for others before I had earned the privilege of working for myself, and I have no doubt that was my great instruction and introduction into Physical Science.'

So Faraday always realized and stressed the importance of carrying out practical experiments and tests. For him the only true scientist was the one who experimentally checked and re-checked his ideas before trying to explain them with a theory.

One surprising thing about Faraday was that although he became one of the greatest scientists who ever lived he was very poor at mathematics. He often had to admit this to other scientists. He explained that he was 'unfortunate in a want of mathematical knowledge'. A year after criticizing his friend Ampère for not carrying out enough practical work, Faraday had to admit to him that he could not follow a particular research paper. 'My deficiencies in mathematical knowledge make me dull in comprehending these subjects,' he wrote. But he was not ashamed of his difficulty and openly confessed his 'want of mathematical knowledge' to another scientist, De La Rio, a few years later.

Despite this weakness in mathematics, Faraday, through his commitment to scientific method, made an enormous contribution to our knowledge and understanding in both chemistry and physics.

Faraday believed that children should be taught science. He started a series of Christmas lectures for children at the Royal Institution in 1827.

7 ▽ Using Faraday's Discoveries Today

Michael Faraday, the son of a blacksmith, the boy who started work delivering newspapers and books, became one of the greatest scientists of all time. During his life the people of Britain thought so highly of him that Parliament awarded him a special pension in thanks for his work and discoveries. Queen Victoria provided a house for him and his wife at Hampton Court where he lived until his death, in 1867, at the age of seventy-six.

Faraday's house at Hampton Court, given to him by Queen Victoria.

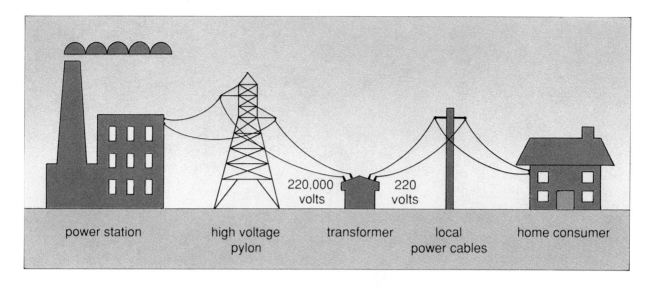

```
power station        high voltage        transformer        local          home consumer
                     pylon                                  power cables
          220,000                220
           volts                 volts
```

We owe a debt of gratitude to this quiet, gentle but proud man. Because of his discovery of benzene we can produce many perfumes, dyes and medicines. We also have to remember him for heat-proof glass and for carbon tetrachloride. But these were small discoveries for Faraday. His reputation and fame have come from his work with electricity and his invention of the electric motor, the transformer and the dynamo.

We have many different types of power station: oil-fired, coal-fired, hydroelectric, wind-powered and nuclear-powered. But they all have one thing in

Above Our modern power supplies depend on two of Faraday's discoveries in electricity: the generator and the transformer.

Left At the International Inventions Exhibition in 1885, electricity was used to illuminate the fountains.

common: to produce electricity they use large dynamos or generators. Michael Faraday's invention is the basis for all the electricity supplied through the power points in our homes, offices, shops and factories.

To get the electricity from the power stations to the houses, offices and factories the supply has to be stepped down from the high voltage at the generators

Sellafield power station in England uses nuclear fuel to produce steam to drive its generators, modern developments from Faraday's dynamo.

to the 240 or 110 volt supplies used domestically and for industry. To do this requires transformers, another of Michael Faraday's inventions.

Almost every appliance that moves requires his third invention, the electric motor.

So every time you switch on a television or radio with their transformers inside them, or travel in a car, bus, train or aeroplane with their motors and dynamos, use a vacuum cleaner, washing machine, or food mixer, or play a cassette, a video or record, you should thank the bookbinder from Newington, the great experimentalist, Michael Faraday.

The CD player, a recent development which relies on Faraday's work.

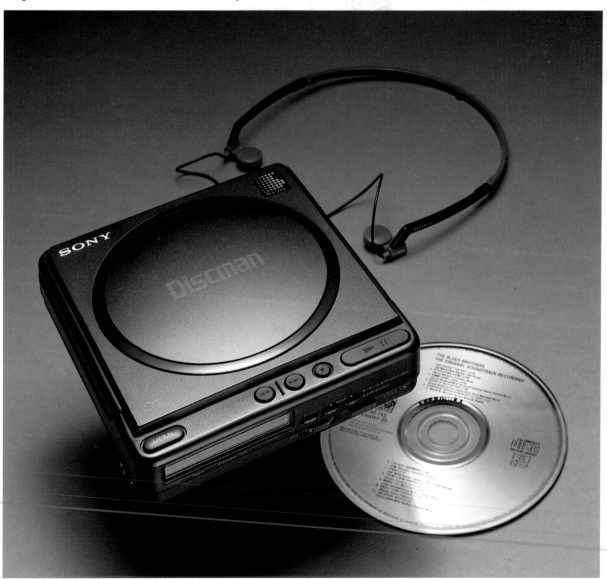

An engraving of Michael Faraday from a popular book on the history of science published at the end of the nineteenth century. The picture shows him apprenticed as a bookbinder (top left) engaged in experiments in his laboratory (top right) and giving a Friday evening lecture at the Royal Institution (bottom).

Date Chart

1791   Michael Faraday born in the village of Newington.

1804   Leaves school at age 13. Starts work as message boy in a book and newspaper shop.

1805   Starts apprenticeship as a bookbinder.

1808   Begins to attend lectures and talks on science.

1812   Becomes a qualified bookbinder.

1813   Appointed as an assistant technician to Davy at the Royal Institution.
(October) Sets off on scientific tour of Europe with Davy and his wife. Meets leading scientists.

1814   Visits Vesuvius in Italy.

1815   Returns with Davy to Britain and continues work at the Royal Institution.

1816   Gives his first lecture at the Royal Institution.

1820   Discovers carbon tetrachloride.

1821   Marries Sarah Barnard, the sister of a friend.

1823   Elected to the French Academy of Sciences.

1824   Discovers benzene and begins work which leads to his invention of heat-proof glass.

1830   Discovers the principle of the electric motor.

1831   (August) Discovers the principle of the transformer.
(October) Discovers the principle of the dynamo.

1832   Proves electricity is the same no matter what its source. Investigates oatmeal fraud for the Royal Navy.

1836   Appointed as Scientific Adviser to Trinity House.

1840   Appointed an elder of his Church.

1844   Dismissed as elder of his Church for dining with Queen Victoria on a Sunday.

1860   Reappointed as elder of Church.

1867   Dies on 25 August at house provided by Queen Victoria at Hampton Court.

Picture acknowledgements

Barnaby's Picture Library 29, 44; Mary Evans Picture Library 7, 12, 13, 21, 22, 40; Michael Holford 16, 18, 33, 34, 38; Billie Love 14, 15; National Portrait Gallery cover; Ann Ronan Picture Library iii, 4, 5, 6, 8, 9, 17, 20, 26, 27, 28, 32, 35 (top), 36, 37, 41, 42, 45; Royal Institution/Wayland Picture Library 23, 24; Wayland Picture Library 11, 25, 28, 43; Zefa 19, 29, 35 (lower). Diagrams on pages 30, 31, 42 are by Jenny Hughes. Cover artwork by Gill Andrae-Reid.

Glossary

Alloy A metal substance made of a mixture of two or more metals, or of a metal and a non-metal.

Ampere (amp) The standard international unit of electric current.

Atmospheric pressure The 'weight' of the air pressing down on to the surface of the Earth.

Barometer The instrument used for measuring atmospheric pressure.

Carbon tetrachloride A colourless liquid with a very sweet smell. It is used in fire extinguishers, some refrigerators and for dry-cleaning.

Chemistry The science which deals with how substances are made up and how they act under different conditions.

Chlorine A greenish-yellow poisonous gas with a very choking or 'pungent' smell.

Compound A substance made up of other elements or substances which have been chemically joined together.

Electromagnet A piece of soft iron that becomes magnetic when an electric current is passed through wire coiled round it.

Electromagnetic induction The production of an electric or magnetic state in a body by bringing another magnetized or electrified body near to it.

Electroplate To coat one metal with a thin layer of another (such as silver).

Focus The point where rays of light are brought together by a lens.

Hydroelectricity Electrical energy obtained from dynamos or generators that are turned by water power.

Iodine A bluish-black solid which is a non-metallic element.

Nuclear energy The energy we can obtain from certain radioactive chemicals such as uranium.

Physics The science which deals with the study of matter and energy, heat, light and sound.

Platinum A soft silvery-white metal which is very resistant to heat and chemicals.

Theory A suggested or possible explanation of something which has been observed.

Transformer A machine or device for changing electric energy from one voltage to another.

Volt The standard unit for measuring the strength of a battery or of an electric power source.

Books to Read

Discovering Electricity by Neil Ardley (Franklin Watts, 1984)

Electricity and Magnetism by Kathryn Whyman (Franklin Watts, 1986)

Exploring Magnets by Ed Catherall (Wayland, 1989)

Focus on Electricity by Mark Lambert (Wayland, 1988)

Michael Faraday and Electricity by Brian Bowers (Wayland, 1977)

The Universal Forces by Peter Lafferty (Wayland, 1990)

The Young Scientist's Book of Electricity by P. Chapman (Usborne, 1976)

Index